Patriotism

and the American Land

Essays by
Richard Nelson
Barry Lopez
Terry Tempest Williams

a publication of The Orion Society

Patriotism and the American Land
by Richard Nelson, Barry Lopez,
and Terry Tempest Williams

ISBN 0-913098-61-2
Copyright © 2002 by The Orion Society

The Orion Society
187 Main Street, Great Barrington, MA 01230
telephone: 413/528-4422   facsimile: 413/528-0676
email: orion@orionsociety.org   website: www.oriononline.org

Cover photograph "Antenna Flag" by Jason Houston
from the documentary series, *Reactions*,
exploring patriotism in the New York area
in the year following September 11, 2001.

Printed on New Leaf Reincarnation Matte paper.
100% recycled, 50% post-consumer, process chlorine free.
Printed in the U.S.A. by Excelsior Printing Co.

2nd printing

Patriotism and the American Land

Foreword

Terrorism. Homeland Security. Patriotism. Since September 11, 2001, these terms have emerged as a fundamental part of our cultural lexicon, with their unsaid assumptions and attendant emotions being used to inspire and buttress a varied set of cultural, political, and military responses to the events of that tragic day.

In the months since that seminal moment in our nation's history, like most Americans we have been deeply immersed in a process of reflection and an ongoing review of the words and actions of our leaders, our media, and our fellow citizens. On many occasions and in different contexts we have been moved to ask the following questions. What is terrorism? What does a secure homeland look like? Who is a patriot?

In response to the September 11 events, The Orion

Society posted a series on OrionOnline called "Thoughts on America: Writers Respond To Crisis." The powerful and heartfelt response to that series led to our publishing a book called *In The Presence of Fear: Three Essays for a Changed World* by Wendell Berry last December.

In late April 2002, we convened a symposium in Eugene, Oregon, to honor writer Barry Lopez with the John Hay Award of The Orion Society. Nearly forty writers and artists of note attended that meeting—"The Literary and Artistic Response to Terrorism"—which culminated in a public event held at the University of Oregon.

Through these efforts, and our travels to communities across our country, we have encountered innumerable citizens who, deeply affected by the horror, implications, and repercussions of September 11, are searching for greater authenticity in the questions and answers about the meaning and significance of that day. In every place, we have spoken with people who, though instinctively wishing to be supportive of our country's leadership during such a traumatic time, are nonetheless deeply disturbed by certain actions undertaken, laws enacted, and statements made in recent months.

As Berry states in *In the Presence of Fear,* "the substitution of rhetoric for thought, always a temptation in a national crisis, must be resisted by officials and citizens alike. It is hard for ordinary citizens to know what is actually happening in Washington in a time of such great trouble; for all we know, serious and difficult thought may be taking place there. But the talk that we are hearing from politicians, bureaucrats, and commentators has so far tended to reduce the complex problems now facing us to issues of unity, security, normality, and retaliation."

Nowhere is this concern more apparent than in the areas of civil liberties, unilateralism in foreign policy, the environment, and public health. This book focuses its discussion primarily on the latter two.

In the months since September 11, respected nonprofit organizations like the Natural Resources Defense Council and Worldwatch★ have kept updated lists of actions undertaken by the current administration on matters of environmental and community health. A review of these lists is troubling, particularly as they seem to demonstrate little governmental regard for, indeed an outright hostility toward, wise stewardship practices. Here are some of the most disturbing examples:

- Outright rejection of internationally negotiated treaties that seek to reduce the threat of global warming combined with aggressive new plans to increase domestic drilling for fossil fuels.

- Broad array of actions to open previously protected public lands—national monuments, wildlife refuges, and national forests—to oil and natural gas drilling, as well as coal and other mining.

- Multiple efforts to withdraw and relax protections for endangered salmon, trout and other species threatened with extinction on the land and in the sea.

– Numerous actions that reduce protections against harmful pollutants and pesticides in our water and air, and major cuts in funding for cleanups of severely polluted sites in our communities (e.g., Superfund).

– Significant cuts to programs and agencies that monitor and enforce protections to the environment, as well as cuts in environmental education spending.

– Exclusion of environmental scientists and other experts from key policy meetings that have been dominated by industry representatives (such as the Energy Task Force).

What is the true meaning of patriotism? The three essays in this new book seek, in their own way, to address essential elements of this question. They ask us to reflect on patriotism in an age where the effects of global warming, created in large measure by human consumption of fossil fuels, are becoming more graphic by the year, when a quarter of the world species are on the brink of extinction, when the number and concentration of toxic chemicals in our communities and our bodies are increasing at a startling rate, and when unrestrained sprawl homogenizes our landscapes and chokes off crucial habitat. The essayists also offer a moving historical and testimonial account of true patriotism, and champion several great American patriots, some well known, others not.

In the first essay, "Patriots for the American Land,"

Richard Nelson eloquently explores the spirit within the conservation movement and argues for an enlightened form of patriotism, where "we are united in a passionate belief that—within the limits of law, morality, and nonviolence—we will defend the health, richness, fecundity, and natural diversity of our nation." Conservationists, he explains, are "patriots for the American land. We are creating, as did the Native Americans long before us, a patriotism based on ecological knowledge, moral consideration, ethical principle, spiritual belief, and a profound love for the earth underfoot."

Barry Lopez, in the second essay, insightfully reviews the evolving role of the "naturalist" over the past two centuries and discusses how "the modern naturalist, acutely aware of the planet's shrinking and eviscerated habitats, often feels compelled to do more than merely register the damage." If we want to be patriotic Americans, Lopez urges us in essence to become a culture of naturalists who "recognize that a politics with no biology, or a politics without field biology, or a political platform in which human biological requirements form but one plank, is a vision of the gates of Hell."

In the concluding essay, Terry Tempest Williams illuminates the character, motivations, creativity, and courage of an exemplary patriot, Rachel Carson. Williams concludes by saying that, as Carson's life and struggle bear out, "There are many forms of terrorism. Environmental degradation is one of them. We have an opportunity to shift the emphasis on American independence to American interdependence and redefine what acts of responsibility count as heroism...perhaps this is what the idea of 'homeland security' is meant to be in times of terror."

The events of September 11 laid bare the souls of nearly every American citizen. Rising out of the desolation of smoke and rubble and loss, we experienced also an unassailable spirit of hope, and with it a palpable expectation of transformation—an opportunity for our souls to deepen, our compassion to grow, and for a new awareness to infuse itself into daily life. These qualities could be seen etched into the faces of nearly every New Yorker one passed on the street in Manhattan for months after the tragedy, and heard in the frequent refrain shared among strangers, "Are you and your family all right?" It was a hope and an expectation that was epitomized by the heroic actions of our rescue workers, and the many other citizens who stood up that day, and since, to be counted.

Have we, a year later, lived up to that powerful sense of expectation? Have we evolved?

If we love America, truly love America, then we—each and every one of us—has a responsibility to take care of that which sustains, nurtures and inspires us. This land is our land, from sea to shining sea, and yet we have not been the wisest of caretakers for our home places, our home*land*, our communities. We need a patriotism that reweaves the frayed fabric of our national identity. We need a patriotism that heals our landscapes and communities, respects and upholds our inalienable rights, and sets us on a path of true justice, freedom, and sustainability. And, finally, we need a patriotism that offers to the rest of the world an authentic and visionary example of leadership.

For a short moment in time a window has opened, a rare opportunity to change the course of civilization. Let us grasp it.

—*September, 2002*
Great Barrington, MA

Marion Gilliam   Laurie Lane-Zucker
Chairman   Executive Director

---

* *Readers are urged to visit Natural Resources Defense Council (www.nrdc.org) and Worldwatch (www.worldwatch.org) websites for further details.*

Patriots for the American Land
by Richard Nelson

I live in the Tongass National Forest, a wild American landscape on the coast of southeastern Alaska. This is the place that nurtures and sustains me; the place on which—and for which—I stand; the place where my engagement with democracy is rooted; the place where I have found an unbeckoned and unexpected sense of patriotism.

My hometown of Sitka perches at the edge of Baranof Island, a ragged spine of mountains about a hundred miles long and twenty miles wide, cleaved by forested valleys and fjordlike bays, with swaths of alpine tundra, hanging glaciers, and high, hidden lakes. Among the island's notable inhabitants are about 1,200 grizzly bears, or "brown bears" as they're known locally. This is approximately the same number of grizzlies now estimated to exist in the entire mainland United States, where at least fifty thousand of these great creatures dwelled in pre-Columbian times.

Recently I joined a group of friends for a boat journey along the island's outer coast, and each day we spotted brown bears rambling along the shorelines, foraging belly-deep in grassy meadows, or slipping away into the forest. One afternoon, as we hiked up a long-abandoned mining road, we found a string of keen-edged bear tracks crossing a streamside gravel bar—so fresh you could almost feel the warm, wet paws in them.

Beyond the stream, we entered a forest of tall spruce and hemlock trees with dense underbrush on either side. "Over the years, I've gotten less and less jittery about brown bears," I remarked. "They seem very shy and mostly interested in avoiding us. You seldom hear of one being aggressive toward people."

"Yeah, I feel the same way," my sidekick agreed. "After a while, you just..."

His voice froze, he caught himself in mid-step, and he stabbed a finger toward the trailside thicket. Not more than twenty feet away, screened by a maze of alder trunks, was a swarthy hillock of muscle and fur.

The bear heaved up onto its pillar-legs, listed from side to side, then disappeared amid the clouds of leaves and ferns. I talked loudly to identify us as humans, meaning no trouble but best left alone. The bushes shook, we heard footbeats pounding heavily away, and then came a protracted, reassuring silence. We stood there for a long moment, peering into the forest, and then burst into breathless rehashes of the encounter. Afterward we hiked on up the valley, keeping sharper eyes on the thickets.

Through the rest of that day I couldn't stop thinking about our incredible good fortune—to encounter a truly wild grizzly bear in a truly wild land, at a time when both have become heartbreakingly scarce. To be in a place where nothing at all has vanished from the natural community, where you do not feel the vast, oppressive emptiness of extinction.

The Tongass is the largest of America's 155 national forests, covering 26,500 square miles, an area the size of West Virginia. It is an unimaginably beautiful place containing the most extensive stands of old-growth temperate rainforest left anywhere on earth. And yet this land—with its ancient forests, abundant bears, and seemingly illimitable wildness—has been inhabited and utilized since ancestral Native Americans arrived here many thousands of years ago. The cultures of their descendants—Tlingit, Haida, and Tsimshian Indians—are a living presence in Tongass communities today.

This long history of intensive habitation by native people is found not only in the Tongass National Forest but throughout Alaska. And still today, most of the state remains utterly pristine, on a massive, spectacular, almost dreamlike scale. This is why sweeping tracts of the Alaskan terrain have been protected as American public wildlands. For example, Alaska's 13 national parks make up 70 percent of the 80 million acres in the entire national park system, and this one state contains more than half of all the designated Wilderness acreage in the U.S.

What I've just said about the Tongass National Forest is also true for the rest of Alaska: apart from the Steller's sea cow—an anomalous manatee-like creature exterminated by Russian hunters in the 1700s—every species of animal and plant known to have existed here before Europeans arrived is still present, and most are not significantly diminished in numbers. In Alaska we have the privilege of bearing witness to the world exactly as God (or the Great Raven of Native Alaskan creation stories) intended it to be, the world complete and intact, making Alaska the rarest of all American treasures and a brilliant source of hope for our future.

The Roots of American Patriotism

How is it that Alaska has been inhabited and used by people for millennia, yet the land remains so lavish and beautiful? We may find the answer by looking at the traditional culture and lifeways of indigenous people like the Koyukon Indians, with whom I spent several years as an anthropologist learning about their relationships to the natural world. There are eleven Koyukon villages scattered over a huge territory along the Yukon and Koyukuk Rivers, just south of the Arctic Circle in the boreal forest of interior Alaska. Although they avail themselves of such modern technology as snowmachines, rifles, and telephones, Koyukon villagers still follow many customary ways—hunting moose, caribou, and black bear; trapping beaver, lynx, fox, and other furbearers; fishing for salmon, whitefish, and northern pike; gathering edible plants and berries.

For Koyukon people, nature is more than a source of food, more than a wellspring of beauty, more than a place to carry out subsistence activities. The living world is also a congregation of sensitive, conscious, spiritually powerful beings. Once, as we trekked along a trail through the wildland, an elder named Lavine Williams told me:

*The country knows. If you do wrong things to it
the whole country knows. It feels what's happening
to it. I guess everything is connected together
somehow, under the ground.*

According to Koyukon tradition, every animal—no matter how large or small—has its own kind of spirit, and the same is true for the trees and all the other plants, for the mountains and valleys, the lakes and rivers, the weather and sky. Elders like Lavine teach a multitude of specific rules which are intended to show courtesy, deference, and humility toward each of these beings. Acting disrespectfully can bring bad luck in hunting, fishing, or gathering; and in serious cases the offender (or a family member) might become sick or even die.

For example, Lavine told me dozens of ways to honor the remains of a bear after it has been killed, and he explained that bears allow themselves to be taken by hunters who are consistently respectful toward their kind. In other words, a bear hunter is successful because he keeps himself in a state of grace with the animals. Lavine also warned that no one should ever insult bears, brag about his hunting exploits, or talk openly of plans to hunt for bears. It is even best to avoid speaking of the bear by name, so Koyukon people often use oblique words like "Black Thing" for a black bear or "Big Animal" for the quintessentially potent grizzly.

To underscore the power and omniscience of these creatures, Lavine advised me: "Always remember this. The bear knows way more than you do."

Another expression of the affiliation between Koyukon people and the land is an assemblage of names—hundreds of names—braided into the terrain, names rich in meaning and memory, names expressing and supporting the Koyukon lifeway, names like *Sis Dlila'*: Black Bear Mountain; *Dolbatno'*: River of the Fledgling Geese; *Ni tsee Ha Daal onh Din*: Wolverine Deadfall Place; *T 'uh Kkokk'a*: Lake of the Short-Bladed Grass; *Saakkay Naalnonh Din*: Place Where the Children Died; *Notozaat Dinh*: Lake Shaped Like a Fishhook; *Dots'on Da'oyh Dinh*: Place of the Nesting Raven; *Nododil Ghun*: Fish Resting Place; *Toti K'its'ikaayh Din*: Where They Shoot Arrows Over the Hill; and the querying name, *Dibaa Dlila*: Whose Mountain?

Traditional Koyukon villagers possess a remarkably intimate, voluminous, and sophisticated knowledge of their surrounding environment. They maintain complex ecological, economic, spiritual, ethical, personal, and social relationships with the natural world. In the Koyukon view, humans and nature comprise one great community, bound together through principles of moral reciprocity, respect, and restraint.

In myriad ways, in ways that lie beyond conscious thought, in ways encompassing both science and spirituality, in ways that may lie beyond an outsider's grasp—Koyukon people understand how their lives are connected with the homeland. Through the processes of hunting, fishing, and gathering their own food, they come to recognize that their bodies are made from the animals and plants they eat, and ultimately from the earth itself. This helps to explain why they feel a strong allegiance toward the land and an obligation to treat it responsibly. In Koyukon tradition, the proper role of humankind is obedience toward the natural world and service toward the environment that gives them life—very different from the western conceit of dominion over nature, and a considerable step beyond the idea of stewardship, which also implies a measure of human control.

As far as I know, every Native American tradition is connected to the homeland and to the natural world in ways similar to those I have described for the Koyukon Indians. Chief Joseph, leader of the Nez Perce Indians, expressed it in the following words: "The earth and myself are of one mind. The measure of the land and the measure of our bodies are the same." Sentiments like these, offered in many native voices over many generations, should be recognized as the bedrock of American patriotism and the foundation for a human commitment to stand in defense of the earth.

ALLEGIANCE AND ACTIVISM

The Tongass National Forest has not been treated as conscientiously as the Koyukon homeland farther north, despite the fact that the Tongass is one of America's most exquisite remaining tracts of wild land. In fact, if this mosaic of islands and fjords, mountains and glaciers, rivers and forests were located in any other state than Alaska, it probably would not be a national forest at all— it would be one of our most revered national parks.

More than a million acres of Tongass rainforest have been destroyed by industrial clearcut logging; some 4,500 miles of logging roads snake into the wildlands; and chainsaws still blare among the ancient, mossy, sighing trees. Tongass clearcutting is planned and managed by the U.S. Forest Service, and the logging itself is done by private timber companies who make bids for the trees. Because these logging operations are unprofitable, they have been underwritten by millions of dollars in taxpayer subsidies each year. (I should mention that large tracts of adjoining lands privately owned by Tlingit and Haida Indian tribal corporations have also been clearcut.)

Destruction of Tongass rainforests and the cost to American taxpayers have brought resistance from throughout the country, and especially from people who live in southeastern Alaska. Over the past twenty years, I have joined the effort to change Tongass logging practices, by supporting many national environmental organizations and, most importantly, by volunteering in my own community for the Sitka Conservation Society, a highly engaged and effective group dedicated to protecting the forest and all that lives in it, including people.

A summary of Sitka Conservation Society activities would sound familiar to anyone involved with grassroots environmental activism. We study Forest Service logging plans, then submit written comments and testify about the plans at public hearings. We meet with congressional delegates, national and regional Forest Service representatives, state government officials, city representatives, and members of other conservation groups. We file lawsuits and submit testimony to the courts. We work to educate local residents and visitors about the forest, its importance to our economy and lifeway, and the ecological consequences of clearcut logging. We encourage a transition to small-scale, selective, ecologically sustainable timber cutting and local wood processing. And we also support a wide range of other nondestructive forest uses, such as tourism, recreation, outdoors education, and scientific research, as well as subsistence hunting, fishing, and gathering.

Conservation work can be rewarding and inspiring, but it's also difficult, exhausting, and sometimes futile. Frustrated activists may grow intensely critical of our society and our government, but this overlooks the fact that we have many reasons to be thankful. Most importantly, as citizens we can significantly influence decisions that will drastically affect the environment around our community and throughout the national forest. Active involvement has given me a source of hope and has fundamentally changed the way I look at America.

During the sixties, I marched and protested against the Vietnam war, the denial of civil rights, and the abuses of corporate-industrial privilege. In my heart, I'm still marching and protesting for many of the same reasons, still acutely aware of my country's problems and shortcomings. Like many others of my generation, the idea of "patriotism" has not rested comfortably in my soul...at least not until recently.

I now see that our conservation work is intricately engaged with, and dependent upon, the process of democracy. I see that every meeting, every written comment, every day in court, every letter to the editor, every newspaper article, every public testimony, every conversation with leaders and officials and neighbors, every ballot initiative, every act of advocacy and protest—every one of these things—is a manifestation of our freedom to speak, to influence decisions, to affect government policies, to educate voters, and above all to change the way our society behaves toward its environment.

With my own eyes, I can see the results of our work: whole mountainsides, broad valleys, and sprawling islands covered with lush, living forest. Places that would have become barrenlands of stumps and slash if we had not used our voices. And if we did not live in a nation where people speaking for the land can be heard. Activists in many other countries have far less opportunity, or no opportunity at all, to influence what happens to their environment. Because of this, I've become grateful for our democratic process (despite all its imperfections) and for our freedom to speak out.

Over the years, conservationists working on behalf of the Tongass National Forest have celebrated each hard-won decision giving protection to another tract of forest—safeguarding habitat for brown bears and bald eagles, for salmon that throng into the spawning streams each summer, and for people who come to hunt and fish, to hike and camp, to find solitude and revitalize their souls. After these victories, especially those that have taken decades of concerted effort with support from literally thousands of people all over the country, my gratitude has bloomed to pure elation.

Whenever conservation activism succeeds in protecting our environment and our health, I feel grateful to live in a country where such achievements are possible. And I feel a growing sense of patriotism. By this I do not mean zealous loyalty toward a flag, veneration for a governmental system, or blind faith in "my country right or wrong." I am simply acknowledging the blessed good fortune to live in a democracy, a place where citizens can substantively influence decisions affecting society and land. And I am expressing my growing sense of allegiance to this living nation.

Allegiance to the forests, the prairies, the deserts, the mountains, the swamplands, the seacoasts, the lakes and rivers and oceans.

Allegiance to the gardens, the wheat fields, the dairy farms, and the range lands from which our bodies are made each day.

Allegiance to long-leaf pine and turkeyfoot bluestem, to field cricket and firefly, to click beetle and carpenter moth, to spadefoot toad and spotted salamander, to desert tortoise and diamondback rattlesnake, to pied-billed grebe and pileated woodpecker, to rufous hummingbird and rough-legged hawk, to meadow vole and muskrat, to black-tailed deer and buffalo and brown bear.

Allegiance to the greater community of landscape and organisms that encompasses and sustains us all.

A NEW PATRIOTISM

"As a true patriot," wrote Henry David Thoreau in his celebrated essay, "Walking," "I should be ashamed to think that Adam in paradise was more favorably situated on the whole than the backwoodsman in this country." In this way, the Walden philosopher expressed patriotic allegiance not just to a system of government but also to the American land itself.

A hundred and fifty years later, Admiral Hyman Rickover echoed Thoreau's land-centered patriotism, but now emphasizing darker concerns: "There is a need for wider recognition that government has as much a duty to protect the land, the air, the water, the natural environment against technological damage, as it has to protect the country against foreign enemies."

My well-worn dictionary defines patriotism as "Devotion to one's country." And a patriot, according to the same authority, is "One who loves his country and zealously guards its welfare." Conservationists fit comfortably into these definitions. We are united in a passionate belief that—within the limits of law, morality, and nonviolence—we will defend the health, richness, fecundity, and natural diversity of our nation.

In other words, I have come to believe that the rapidly growing community of citizens who care deeply about our country's natural heritage—and who are working to celebrate, sustain, and protect this heritage—should be regarded as patriots for the American land.

We are creating, as did the Native Americans long before us, a patriotism based on ecological knowledge, moral consideration, ethical principle, spiritual belief, and a profound love for the earth underfoot. I believe this is the most basic, most urgent, and most vital patriotism of all, because conservationists are working in service to the elemental roots of their existence, as human organisms, as members of their communities, and as citizens of their nation's land.

To what extent do America's political leaders embrace this fundamental patriotism toward the American land? Sadly, the present national administration and congress are predominantly antagonistic toward policies that protect the biological integrity and economic sustainability of our environment. Americans concerned about the environment must strengthen their collective voice and enlarge their constituency. To do this, I believe they should acclaim their patriotism, their allegiance to the American land, and their gratitude for the privileges of democracy and free speech.

It seems ironic that conservation has become associated in America with progressive politics rather than with political conservatism. After all, conservation is fundamentally conservative. Both words share a common root; both urge respect for old, established traditions; and both advocate moving slowly, cautiously. Back to the dictionary for this definition of conservative: "Inclined to preserve the existing order of things...Conserving; preservative."

Where I live, as in many other parts of the rural west, "environmentalist" can be a nasty word, an insult, an accusation. Not surprisingly, some of us prefer to call ourselves "conservationists"—a better word in any case, because it acknowledges that we must use the earth while emphasizing that we should do it responsibly. Conservatively.

Conservationists can frustrate even their closest friends when they self-righteously ignore or overlook their own dependence on the industries they criticize. Just to keep it safe, I'll implicate only myself. How could I oppose all logging when I live in a house built of wood and my work depends on paper made from trees? How could I oppose all drilling for oil when I travel by car, airplane, and motor powered boat? How could I oppose all mining when I use so many wonderful items made from steel, copper, and aluminum?

Clear and simple as these observations may be, they are often ignored in the rhetoric of conservation, and they are just as often pointed out by critics of environmentalism. Informed activists should acknowledge their participation in the industrial system, their own culpability, their own personal ecology. For southeast Alaska conservationists, this means finding a balance between criticism and advocacy. We oppose logging that destroys whole biological communities, in a place where it takes at least two centuries to restore a functioning old-growth forest. But we advocate for small-scale, ecologically sustainable logging which can provide wood while keeping the forest community—and the long-term economy—intact.

Informed activism also comes down to personal choices, like remembering that every lumber purchase amounts to a "yes" vote for the sort of logging that produced the wood. Sustainably harvested lumber can be hard to find and might cost a bit more, but it's essential to support businesses that are committed to using the forest responsibly and to acknowledge the work of those who produce ethically grounded materials.

The same principles apply to mining, oil drilling, farming, ranching, and manufacturing. It's imperative to remember that all of us take from the earth, even if someone else digs, fells, harvests, kills, builds, and processes on our behalf. Every moment of our lives is a gift from the land and from the people who labor on it. When we support responsible uses of the environment, it lends credibility to our protests against destructive uses; uses that violate the integrity of the American land; uses that may justifiably be characterized as unpatriotic.

PUBLIC LANDS AND AMERICAN DEMOCRACY

One of the most important commitments the American people have made is to set a part of our nation aside as public land—where everyone has equal access, equal opportunity to find sustenance for their souls, equal responsibility as a stakeholder and caretaker, and equal freedom to roam across the American earth.

We all know that America's public lands "belong" to every citizen. But does this actually register in our minds at a deep, intuitive level? Most of us consider ourselves owners of the little parcels we live on; or, lacking that, as owners of nothing at all. When people around the country are dismayed to learn that the Tongass National Forest is being clearcut, do they think: "Hey, wait a minute, I own that place!"? Many Americans are inclined to say public land belongs to "the government," but it's essential to remember that in this country the government is us.

If people thought of themselves as the real owners of these American places, they'd probably care more about them, do more to support them, and take more action to defend them. American public lands are the paragon and epitome of our democratic society, one of this country's greatest achievements—a triumphant legacy that we have given to ourselves, to our children, and to the world.

And yet there is a growing movement to take this land—piece by piece—away from us. Some powerful members of the U.S. Congress are passionately committed to getting our American public lands into private ownership, or failing that, to maximize private commercial and industrial uses of these lands. They launch bill after bill, rider after rider, to carve parcels of every size out of the national wildlands, or to promote intense extractive uses within their boundaries.

These same politicians and their supporters also vow that no more of the American land will be "locked up" in public ownership. But is it not true that private land is the ultimate lockup? After all, our American public lands are open to everyone, and far from being unused, these are among the most intensely utilized places in our country. A few of these uses include hiking, camping, wildlife watching, horseback riding, kayaking, photographing, swimming, bicycling, climbing, skiing, teaching, researching, hunting, fishing, finding good company or solitude, restoring health or fitness, rejuvenating soul and spirit, bringing the history, culture, and wild heritage of this nation into ourselves.

Consider the case of Alaska. Well over a million tourists travel to this state every year—drawn perhaps above all else by the beauty and wildness of Alaska's national public lands, and by the dream of seeing majestic animals like the grizzly bear my friends and I encountered in the Tongass National Forest that summer day. For many people, seeing a grizzly in the wild is a true lifetime experience. But on a few Tongass islands, there is something more to consider as well.

Recent DNA studies show that the brown bears, or grizzlies, of Baranof Island (where I live) and two neighboring islands—Admiralty and Chichagof—are profoundly different from all other grizzly bears in North America. These island bears have been separated from other bear populations for many thousands of years and have changed relatively little from their closest kin, the brown bears of Asia. According to biologists, there are two kinds of brown or grizzly bears in the world: first, those living on Baranof, Admiralty, and Chichagof Islands, and second, all the others.

Even more surprising, the bears of these three islands are closer to the polar bear on the family tree of ursine genetics than they are to any of the brown or grizzly bears. And thanks to Theodore Roosevelt's designation of the Tongass National Forest in 1902, these singular creatures are living today on public land, where all of the American people can see and appreciate them, speak on their behalf, and act as their stewards.

PATRIOTISM AND THE AMERICAN LAND

Discovering the uniqueness of Tongass island bears, which happened about fifteen years ago, reminds us that our national lands are filled with hidden treasures. We can be certain that every tract of public wildland in our country harbors its own secrets, yet to be revealed. A part of our responsibility is to preserve the places where these secrets live, and to give our descendents the same chance to explore and discover the lands we bequeath to them.

It seems like a miracle that places like these still exist at the beginning of the twenty-first century. I believe we should treat America's public wildlands with the same reverence we give to our treasured national shrines and edifices—the Statue of Liberty, the Smithsonian Institution, the Lincoln Memorial, the Alamo, the Mesa Verde ruins, the St. Louis Arch, the Washington Monument.

We should honor our American public lands, celebrate them, study them, teach our children about them, find hope and solace in them, restore and enrich them, and enlarge them at every opportunity. We should remember their names as places worthy of special allegiance—names like Klamath National Forest, Haleakala National Park, Cape Cod National Seashore, Denali National Park, Chickasaw National Wildlife Refuge, Fire Island National Seashore, Los Padres National Forest, Organ Pipe Cactus National Monument, Glen Canyon National Recreation Area, Arctic National Wildlife Refuge, Chequamegan National Forest, Rainbow Bridge National Monument, Sleeping Bear Dunes National Seashore, Siuslaw National Forest, Big Bend National Park.

For me, there are many reasons to be a patriot for the American land:

First, protecting the land is nothing less than protecting ourselves, our children, our communities, our nation. After all, our bodies are made in large measure from the soil of this continent; and from the waters; and from the plants and animals these soils and waters nourish. Where our environment is kept clean and vital, its cleanliness and vitality flows through us. Again, I remember Chief Joseph's words: "The measure of the land and the measure of our bodies are the same."

Second, allegiance to the land is allegiance to our community as a whole. I believe we have a moral and ethical obligation to protect this living community, to use it responsibly, and to support the work of educating every citizen about the natural environment, the cultural values, and the historical events that give such richness to our American national lands.

Third, standing up for protection of the American land is a way to give something back in return for the gifts of sustenance and beauty and living enrichment that they have given to us. I believe in the importance of tithing—of giving service on behalf of the land and all that lives on it. This is based on a sense of reciprocity and obligation that has deep roots in many Native American traditions. "Take care of the land," I once heard a Tlingit Indian elder say, "and the land will take care of you."

Fourth, working in service to the land is a powerful source of hope—the kind of hope that comes by doing something rather than standing by in the face of loss. By this I mean working to protect both the natural environment and the human traditions that infuse every place with power and meaning. There is real joy in this work, especially because it brings us into the company of like-minded people who support each other in the rough times and share the rewards when things go well.

I am still keenly aware of our country's flaws and shortcomings; still frustrated by its inability to find balance with the environment. But I am grateful for the freedom to speak out, grateful to live in a nation where I can work on behalf of the land, grateful for the gift of hope, grateful for the privilege of sharing my chosen home with grizzly bears, in a magnificent forest of ancient, sheltering trees.

All these things make me proud to say that I am a patriot for the American land.

> I pledge allegiance to the soil
> of Turtle Island,
> and to the beings who thereon dwell
>> one ecosystem
>> in diversity
>> under the sun
> With joyful interpenetration for all.

—Gary Snyder

THE NATURALIST

by Barry Lopez

My home stands on a wooded bench, set back about two hundred feet from the north bank of the McKenzie River in western Oregon. Almost every day I go down to the river with no intention but to sit and watch. I have been watching the river for thirty years, just the three or four hundred yards of it I can see from the forested bank, a run of clear, quick water about 350 feet wide. If I have learned anything here, it's that each time I come down, something I don't know yet will reveal itself.

If it's a man's intent to spend thirty years staring at a river's environs in order to arrive at an explanation of the river, he should find some other way to spend his time. To assert this, that a river can't be known, does not to my way of thinking denigrate science, any more than saying a brown bear can't be completely known. The reason this is true is because the river is not a thing, in the way a Saturn V rocket engine is a thing. It is an expression of biological life, in dynamic relation to everything around it—the salmon within, the violet-green swallow swooping its surface, alder twigs floating its current, a mountain lion sipping its bank water, the configurations of basalt that break its flow and give it timbre and tone.

In my experience with field biologists, those fresh to a task—say, caracara research—are the ones most likely to give themselves a deadline—ten years, say—against which they will challenge themselves to know all there is to know about that falcon. It never works. More seasoned field biologists, not as driven by a need to prove themselves, are content to concentrate on smaller arenas of knowledge. Instead of speaking definitively of coyote, armadillo, or wigeon, they tend to say, "This one animal, that one time, did this in that place." It's the approach to nature many hunting and gathering peoples take, to this day. The view suggests a horizon rather than a boundary for knowing, toward which we are always walking.

A great shift in the Western naturalist's frame of mind over the past fifty years, it seems to me, has been the growth of this awareness: to get anywhere deep with a species, you must immerse yourself in its milieu. You must study its ecology. If you wish to understand the caracara, you need to know a great deal about exactly where the caracara lives when; and what the caracara's relationships are with each of the many components of that place, including its weathers, its elevations, its seasonal light.

A modern naturalist, then, is no longer someone who goes no further than a stamp collector, mastering nomenclature and field marks. She or he knows a local flora and fauna as pieces of an inscrutable mystery, increasingly deep, a unity of organisms Western culture has been trying to elevate itself above since at least Mesopotamian times. The modern naturalist, in fact, has now become a kind of emissary in this, working to reestablish good relations with all the biological components humanity has excluded from its moral universe.

Sitting by the river, following mergansers hurtling past a few inches off its surface or eyeing an otter hauled out on a boulder with (in my binoculars) the scales of a trout glistening on its face, I ask myself not: What do I know?—that Canada geese have begun to occupy the nests of osprey here in recent springs, that harlequin ducks are now expanding their range to include this stretch of the river—but: Can I put this together? Can I imagine the river as a definable entity, evolving in time?

How is a naturalist today supposed to imagine the place between nature and culture? How is he or she to act, believing as many do that Western civilization is compromising its own biology by investing so heavily in material progress? And knowing that many in positions of corporate and political power regard nature as inconvenient, an inefficiency in their plans for a smoothly running future?

The question of how to behave, it seems to me, is

nervewracking to contemplate because it is related to two areas of particular discomfort for naturalists. One is how to keep the issue of spirituality free of religious commentary; the other is how to manage emotional grief and moral indignation in pursuits so closely tied to science, with its historical claim to objectivity.

One response to the first concern is that the naturalist's spirituality is one with no icons (unlike religion's), and it is also one that enforces no particular morality. In fact, for many it is not much more than the residue of awe which modern life has not (yet) erased, a sensitivity to the realms of life which are not yet corraled by dogma. The second concern, how a person with a high regard for objectivity deals with emotions like grief and outrage, like so many questions about the trajectory of modern culture, is only a request to express love without being punished. It is, more deeply, an expression of the desire that love be on an equal footing with power when it comes to social change.

It is of some help here, I think, to consider where the modern naturalist has come from, to trace her or his ancestry. Since the era of Gilbert White in eighteenth-century England, by some reckonings, we have had a recognizable cohort of people who study the natural world and write about it from personal experience. White and his allies wrote respectfully about nature, and their treatments were meant to be edifying for the upper classes. Often, the writer's intent was merely to remind the reader not to overlook natural wonders, which were the evidence of Divine creation. Darwin, in his turn, brought unprecedented depth to this kind of work. He accentuated the need for scientific rigor in the naturalist's inquiries, but he also suggested that certain far-reaching implications existed. Entanglements. People, too, he said, were biological, subject to the same forces of mutation as the finch. A hundred years further on, a man like Aldo Leopold could be characterized as a keen observer, a field biologist who understood a deeper connection (or reconnection) with nature, but also as someone aware of the role wildlife science had begun to play in politics. With Rachel Carson, the artificial but sometimes dramatic divide that can separate the scientist, with her allegiance to objective, peer-reviewed data, from the naturalist, for whom biology always raises issues of propriety, becomes apparent.

Following Leopold's and Carson's generations came a generation of naturalists that combined White's enthusiasm and sense of the nonmaterial world; Leopold's political consciousness and feelings of shared fate; and Carson's sense of rectitude and citizenship. For the first time, however, the humanists among this cadre of naturalists were broadly educated in the sciences. They had grown up with Watson and Crick, not to mention sodium fluoroacetate, Ebola virus ecology, melting ice shelves, and the California condor.

The modern naturalist, acutely even depressingly aware of the planet's shrinking and eviscerated habitats, often feels compelled to do more than merely register the damage. The impulse to protest, however, is often stifled by feelings of defensiveness, a fear of being misread. Years of firsthand field observation can be successfully challenged in court today by a computer modeler with not an hour's experience in the field. A carefully prepared analysis of stream flow, migration corridors, and long-term soil stability in a threatened watershed can be written off by the press (with some assistance from the opposition) as a hatred of mankind.

At the opening of the twenty-first century the naturalist, then, knows an urgency White did not foresee and a political scariness Leopold might actually have imagined in his worst moments. Further, in the light of the still-unfolding lessons of Charles Darwin's work, he or she knows that a cultural exemption from biological imperatives remains in the realm of science fiction.

In contemporary native villages, one might posit today that all people actively engaged in the land—hunting, fishing, gathering, traveling, camping—are naturalists, and say that some are better than others according to their gifts of observation. Native peoples differ here, however, from the Gilbert Whites, the Darwins, the Leopolds, and the Rachel Carsons in that accumulating and maintaining this sort of information is neither avocation nor profession. It is more comparable to religious activity, behavior steeped in tradition and considered essential for the maintenance of good living. It is a moral and an inculcated stance, a way of being. While White and others, by contrast, were searching for a way back *in* to nature, native peoples (down to the present in some instances), for whatever reason, have been at pains not to leave. The distinction is important because "looking for a way back in" is a striking characteristic of the modern naturalist's frame of mind.

Gilbert White stood out among his social peers because what he pursued—a concrete knowledge of the natural world around Selbourne in Hampshire—was unrelated to politics or progress. As such, it could be dismissed politically. Fascinating stuff, but inconsequential. Since then, almost every naturalist has borne the supercilious judgments of various sophisticates who thought the naturalist a romantic, a sentimentalist, a bucolic—or worse; and more latterly, the condescension of some scientists who thought the naturalist not rigorous, not analytic, not detached enough.

A naturalist of the modern era—an experientially based, well-versed devotee of natural ecosystems—is ideally among the best informed of the American electorate when it comes to the potentially catastrophic environmental effects of political decisions. The contemporary naturalist, it has turned out—again, scientifically grounded, politically attuned, field experienced, library enriched—is no custodian of irrelevant knowledge, no mere adept differentiating among *Empidonax* flycatchers on the wing, but a kind of citizen whose involvement in the political process, in the debates of public life, in the evolution of literature and the arts, has become crucial.

The bugbear in all of this—and there is one—is the role of field experience, the degree to which the naturalist's assessments are empirically grounded in firsthand knowledge. How much of what the contemporary naturalist claims to know about animals and the ecosystems they share with humans derives from what he has read, what he has heard, what he has seen televised? What part of what the naturalist has sworn his or her life to comes from firsthand experience, from what the body knows?

One of the reasons native people still living in some sort of close, daily association with their ancestral lands are so fascinating to those who arrive from the rural, urban, and suburban districts of civilization is because they are so possessed of authority. They radiate the authority of firsthand encounters. They are storehouses of it. They have not read about it, they have not compiled notebooks and assembled documentary photographs. It is so important that they remember it. When you ask them for specifics, the depth of what they can offer is scary. It's scary because it's not tidy, it doesn't lend itself to summation. By the very way that they say that they know, they suggest they are still learning something that cannot, in the end, be known.

It is instructive to consider how terrifying certain interlopers—rural developers, government planners, and other apostles of change—can seem to such people when, on the basis of a couple of books the interloper has read or a few (usually summer) weeks in the field with a pair of binoculars and some radio collars, he suggests a new direction for the local ecosystem and says he can't envision any difficulties.

In all the years I have spent standing or sitting on the banks of this river, I have learned this: the more knowledge I have, the greater becomes the mystery of what holds that knowledge together, this reticulated miracle called an ecosystem. The longer I watch the river, the more amazed I become (afraid, actually, sometimes) at the confidence of those people who after a few summer seasons here are ready to tell the county commissioners, emphatically, what the river is, to scribe its meaning for the outlander.

Firsthand knowledge is enormously time consuming to acquire; with its dallying and lack of end points, it is also out of phase with the short-term demands of modern life. It teaches humility and fallibility, and so represents an antithesis to progress. It makes a stance of awe in the witness of natural process seem appropriate, and attempts at summary knowledge naïve. Historically, tyrants have sought selectively to eliminate firsthand knowledge when its sources lay outside their control. By silencing those with problematic firsthand experiences, they reduced the number of potential contradictions in their political or social designs, and so they felt safer. It is because natural process—how a mountain range disintegrates or how nitrogen cycles through a forest—is beyond the influence of the visionaries of globalization that firsthand knowledge of a country's ecosystems, a rapidly diminishing pool of expertise and awareness, lies at the radical edge of any country's political thought.

Over the years I have become a kind of naturalist, although I previously rejected the term because I felt I did not know enough, that my knowledge was far too incomplete. I never saw myself in the guise of Gilbert White, but I respected his work enough to have sought out his grave in Selbourne and expressed there my gratitude for his life. I never took a course in biology, not even in high school, and so it seemed to me that I couldn't really be any sort of authentic naturalist. What biology I was able to learn I took from books, from veterinary clinics, from an apprenticeship to my homeland in the Cascades, from field work with Western biologists, and from traveling with hunters and gatherers. As a naturalist, I have taken the lead of native tutors, who urged me to participate in the natural world, not hold it before me as an object of scrutiny.

When I am by the river, therefore, I am simply there. I watch it closely, repeatedly, and feel myself not apart from it. I do not feel compelled to explain it. I wonder sometimes, though, whether I am responding to the wrong question when it comes to speaking "for nature." Perhaps the issue is not whether one has the authority to claim to be a naturalist, but whether those who see themselves as naturalists believe they have the authority to help shape the world. What the naturalist-as-emissary intuits, I think, is that if he or she doesn't speak out, the political debate will be left instead to those seeking to benefit their various constituencies. Strictly speaking, a naturalist has no constituency.

To read the newspapers today, to merely answer the phone, is to know the world is in flames. People do not have time for the sort of empirical immersion I believe crucial to any sort of wisdom. This terrifies me, but I, too, see the developers' bulldozers arrayed at the mouth of every canyon, poised at the edge of every plain. And the elimination of these lands, I know, will further reduce the extent of the blueprints for undamaged life. After the last undomesticated stretch of land is brought to heel, there will be only records—strips of film and recording tape, computer printouts, magazine articles, books, laser-beam surveys—of these immensities. And then any tyrant can tell us what it meant, and in which direction we should now go. In this scenario, the authority of the grizzly bear will be replaced by the authority of a charismatic who says he represents the bear. And the naturalist—the ancient emissary to a world civilization wished to be rid of, a world it hoped to transform into a chemical warehouse, the same uneasy emissary who intuited that to separate nature from culture wouldn't finally work—will be an orphan. He will become a dealer in myths.

What being a naturalist has come to mean to me, sitting my mornings and evenings by the river, hearing the clack of herons through the creak of swallows over the screams of osprey under the purl of fox sparrows, so far removed from White and Darwin and Leopold and even

Carson, is this: Pay attention to the mystery. Apprentice to the best apprentices. Rediscover in nature your own biology. Write and speak with appreciation for all you have been gifted. Recognize that a politics with no biology, or a politics without field biology, or a political platform in which human biological requirements form but one plank, is a vision of the gates of Hell.

ONE PATRIOT

by Terry Tempest Williams

Not long ago, my father, a friend and I were having tea around our kitchen table. We were discussing politics. The conversation circled back to September 11.

"I hesitate to say this," our friend said. "But when I watched the Twin Towers collapse and realized thousands of lives were collapsing with them—" She paused to find the right words. "It just didn't seem real. I couldn't believe it. And then seeing the hole in the side of the Pentagon and hearing about more lives lost in Pennsylvania, well, it all felt like I was watching some horrific movie—But afterwards in the privacy of my own fears, I realized, living here in the West, what would truly shatter my world would be if the terrorists bombed the Tetons or the Grand Canyon..."

"Nobody could bomb the Tetons—" my father said

interrupting her. "That's ridiculous."

"No, let me finish—," she said. "What I mean to say is that for me, the worst thing terrorists could do would be to destroy these wild places—like the Tetons, Yellowstone, all this redrock country..."

"They are," I said.

My father looked at me and said nothing. We drank our tea.

Kenneth Rexroth writes, "The art of being civilized is the art of learning to read between the lies."

There have been many lies delivered in the name of national security since September 11, 2001. Fear has opened the door to fanaticism. The fabric of our civil liberties has been raveled. Those who raise questions are told to raise American flags instead. A hollow patriotism has emerged. We might as well be blowing "My Country 'Tis of Thee" through plastic kazoos.

Meanwhile, corporate America is imploding through its own greed, the stock market has become a trampoline leaving many investors suspended in midair as Bush II makes plans to attack Iraq and we bomb wedding parties in Afghanistan. The American West is being ravaged by oil and gas companies and federal regulations that have kept our air, water, and wildlife safe are now being erased.

Indeed, we are engaged in a war of terrorism.

Here in Castle Valley, Utah, with temperatures hovering around 110 degrees this summer and the valley filled with smoke from fires burning in Colorado and Arizona, it's easy to become apocalyptic about our future. The sun burns blood red through the haze. My Mormon neighbor reminds me of Proverbs 29:18: "Where there is no vision, the people perish."

But America is still a democracy and a strong one. We do have people with vision. That is our history. And, at this moment, no one looms larger in my mind than Rachel Carson. Here was a wildlife biologist, a government employee who worked for the U.S. Fish and Wildlife Service and with her pen exposed the dangers of the entire chemical industry. It is her spirit I wish to recall and remember now. She is my model for a true patriot, one who not only dared to define democratic principles as ecological ones, but demanded through her grace and fierce intelligence that we hold corporations and our government accountable for the health of our communities, cultured and wild.

Rachel Carson. I first heard her name from my grandmother. I must have been seven or eight years old. We were feeding birds—song sparrows, goldfinches, and towhees—in my grandparents' yard in Salt Lake City.

"Imagine a world without birds," my grandmother said as she scattered seed and filled the feeders. "Imagine waking up to no birdsong."

I couldn't.

"Rachel Carson," I remember her saying.

Later, around the dinner table, she and my grandfather were engaged in an intense discussion of the book they were reading, *Silent Spring,* as my mind tried to grasp what my grandmother had just said about a muted world.

Decades later, I found myself in a used bookstore in Salt Lake City. The green spine of *Silent Spring* caught my eye. I pulled the classic off the shelf and opened it. First edition, 1962. As I read various passages, I was struck by how little had changed. Each page was still a shock and a revelation.

> *One of the most tragic examples of our unthinking bludgeoning of the landscape is to be seen in the sagebrush lands of the West, where a vast campaign is on to destroy the sage and to substitute grasslands. If ever an enterprise needed to be illuminated with a sense of history and meaning of the landscape, it is this.... It is spread before us like the pages of an open book in which we can read why the land is what it is, and why we should preserve its integrity. But the pages lie unread.*

The pages of abuse on the American landscape still lie unread.

Rachel Carson is a hero, a towering example within American democracy of how one person's voice can make an extraordinary difference both in public policy and in the minds of the populace. Her name and her vision of a world intact and interrelated entered mainstream culture in the 1960's, heralding the beginning of the modern conservation movement. Even so, in the year of *Silent Spring*'s fortieth anniversary, I wonder how many of us really know much about Miss Carson's life or have ever read this crucial book?

We can all rattle off a glib two-sentence summation of its text: "All life is connected. Pesticides enter the food chain and not only threaten the environment but destroy it." And yet, I fear that *Silent Spring*'s status as "an American classic" allows us to nod to its power, but to miss the subtleties and richness of the book as both a scientific treatise and a piece of distinguished literary nonfiction.

Rachel Carson presents her discoveries of destruction in the form of storytelling. In example after example, grounded in the natural world, she weaves together facts and fictions into an environmental tale of life, love, and loss. Her voice is forceful and dignified, but sentence by sentence she delivers right hand blows and counter punches to the status quo ruled by chemical companies within the Kingdom of Agriculture.

The "control of nature" is a phrase conceived in arrogance, born of the Neanderthal age of biology and philosophy, when it was supposed that nature exists for the convenience of man…. It is our alarming misfortune that so primitive a science has armed itself with the most modern and terrible weapons, and that in turning them against the insects it has also turned them against the earth.

The facts she presents create the case against "biocide": We are killing the very fabric of nature in our attempt to rid the world of pests through these "elixirs of death." She indicts the insecticides by name: DDT, chlordane, heptachlor, dieldrin, aldrin, and endrin. And then she adds parathion and malathion, organic phosphates that are among the most poisonous chemicals in the world.

The fictions she exposes are the myths we have chosen to adopt in our obsession to control nature. She reminds us of the story of Medea, the Greek sorceress who, overwrought with jealousy over her husband's love of another woman, presents the new bride with a gift, a robe that will immediately kill whoever wears it. It becomes a garment of death. Carson calls our use of pesticides "death by indirection." We are killing insects and in turn, killing ourselves, as these toxins slowly and violently enter the waters and eventually our own bloodstreams.

Rachel Carson did not turn her back on the ongoing chronicle of the natural history of the dead. She bore witness. "It was time," Carson said, "that human beings admit their kinship with other forms of life. If we cannot accept this moral ethic, then we too are complicit in the killing."

With each chapter, she adds to our understanding of the horrors of herbicides and hydrocarbons, the web of life unraveling. It is impossible for us not to be inspired by Rachel Carson's emotional and intellectual stamina, of her ability to endure the pain of the story she was telling.

Miss Carson had a vision.

"Sometimes, I lose sight of my goal," she wrote in an essay in her first year of college. "Then again it flashes into view, filling me with a new determination to keep the vision before my eyes." Hers was a conscientious and directed soul who believed in the eloquence of facts. She loved both language and landscape. "I can remember no time when I wasn't interested in the out-of-doors and the whole world of nature," Carson said.

Writing became the expression for her passion toward nature. She published her first story when she was ten years old, winning the Silver Badge from the prestigious children's magazine, *St. Nicholas*. "Perhaps the early experience of seeing my work in print played its part in fostering my childhood dream of becoming a writer."

Here was a young woman pulled by her destiny. In 1928, she graduated magna cum laude from Pennsylvania College for Women, now Chatham College, with a major in zoology. The strength of her course work in both science and literature supports the evidence of her dual nature as both a scientist and a poet.

"I thought I had to be one or the other," she said. "It never occurred to me that I could combine two careers."

Paul Brooks, Rachel Carson's editor, writes, "The merging of these two powerful currents—the imagination and insight of a creative writer with a scientist's passion for fact—goes far to explain the blend of beauty and authority that was to make her books unique."

Rachel Carson's gift to us is seeing the world whole.

Carson continued her education as a biologist, receiving a master's degree in zoology at Johns Hopkins University, where she studied genetics and wrote her thesis, "The Development of the Pronephros During the Embryonic and Early Larval Life of the Catfish (*Ictalurus punctatus*)."

In 1936, she accepted a position with the United States Bureau of Fisheries, which later became the U.S. Fish & Wildlife Service, as an aquatic biologist. Here she was able to effectively fuse her talents as a scientist and a writer, eventually becoming chief of publications for the bureau. Early in her tenure at Fish & Wildlife, she continued teaching courses at the University of Maryland and Johns Hopkins.

Under the Sea-Wind was published in 1941. *The Sea Around Us* was published in 1951 to great popular and critical acclaim, receiving the National Book Award in nonfiction. It remained on *The New York Times* bestseller list for months. "If there is poetry in my book about the sea," she said, "it is not because I deliberately put it there, but because no one could truthfully write about the sea and leave out the poetry."

In 1955, four years after the success of *The Sea Around Us*, Carson published *The Edge of the Sea*, extending her readers' knowledge of the ocean to the ocean's interface with land. She focused her naturalist's eye on tidepools, writing about the extraordinary nature of adaptation in a littoral world, while at the same time illuminating the magic and intricacies of the sandy beach and rocky shore. Her words not only speak of a natural history but a natural philosophy:

Now I hear the sea sounds about me; the night high tide is rising, swirling with a confused rush of waters against the rocks below my study window... these coastal forms merge

*and blend in a shifting, kaleidescopic pattern in which there is
no finality, no ultimate and fixed reality—earth becoming
fluid as the sea itself.… Contemplating the teeming life of the
shore, we have an uneasy sense of the communication of some
universal truth that lies just beyond our grasp. What is the
message signaled by the hordes of diatoms, flashing their
microscopic lights in the night sea?…The meaning haunts
and ever eludes us, and in its very pursuit we approach the
ultimate mystery of Life itself.*

And then came *Silent Spring.*

Rachel Carson received a letter from her friend Olga
Owens Huckins, a journalist, who asked her for help in
finding people who could elucidate and speak to the
dangers of pesticides. The Huckinses had a small place in
Duxbury, Massachusetts, just north of Cape Cod, which
they had made into a bird sanctuary. Without any
thought of the effects on birds and wildlife, the state had
sprayed the entire area for mosquito control.

Huckins sent a letter of outrage to *The Boston Herald*
in January, 1958. Here is an excerpt:

*The mosquito control plane flew over our small town last
summer. Since we live close to the marshes, we were treated to
several lethal doses as the pilot crisscrossed our place. And we
consider the spraying of active poison over private land to be
a serious aerial intrusion.*

*The 'harmless' shower bath killed seven of our lovely song-
birds outright. We picked up three dead bodies the next*

*morning right by the door. They were birds that had lived
close to us, trusted us, and built their nests in our trees year
after year. The next day three were scattered around the bird
bath. (I had emptied it and scrubbed it after the spraying but
YOU CAN NEVER KILL DDT).*

*...All of these birds died horribly and in the same way.
Their bills were gaping open, and their splayed claws were
drawn up to their breasts in agony.*

Olga Owens Huckins bore witness. Rachel Carson
responded. Four and a half years later in 1962, *Silent
Spring* was published. Carson wrote to Huckins that it
was her letter that had "started it all" and had led her to
realize that "I must write the book."

This was a correspondence between friends, two
women standing their ground in the places they loved,
each one engaging the gifts they possessed to make a
difference in the world. We can never forget the power
of impassioned, informed individuals sharing their stories
of place, bearing witness, speaking out on behalf of the
land they call home.

Rachel Carson told the truth as she understood it. The
natural world was dying, poisoned by the hands of
power tied to corporate greed. Her words became an
open wound in immediate need of attention. A debate
had begun: a reverence for life versus a reverence for
industry. Through the strength and vitality of her voice,
Carson altered the political landscape of America forever.

Loren Eisely wrote that *Silent Spring* "is a devastating,

heavily documented, relentless attack upon human carelessness, greed, and responsibility."

Not everyone saw it that way.

The Monsanto Chemical Company, anticipating the publication of *Silent Spring*, urgently commissioned a parody entitled "The Desolate Year" to counteract Carson's attack on the industry. Its intent was to show the pestilence and famine that Monsanto claimed would occur in a world without pesticides.

Robert White-Stevens, a biochemist who was assistant director of the Agricultural Research Division of American Cyanamid, became the chemical industry's spokesman. He made over twenty-eight speeches against *Silent Spring*. He was outraged by the evidence waged against DDT, charging that Carson was "a fanatic defender of the cult of the balance of nature."

In its weekly newsletter, the American Medical Association told the public how to obtain an "information kit," compiled by the National Agriculture Chemicals Association, to answer questions provoked by *Silent Spring*.

Time magazine called *Silent Spring* "unfair, one-sided, and hysterically over-emphatic," and accused Carson of frightening the public with "emotion-fanning words," claiming her text was filled with "oversimplifications and downright errors."

Former Secretary of Agriculture Ezra Taft Benson (who later became Prophet of the Mormon Church) wrote to Dwight D. Eisenhower regarding Rachel

Carson, asking simply, "Why a spinster with no children was so concerned about genetics?" His own conjecture was that she was "probably a Communist."

Spinster. Communist. A member of a nature cult. An amateur naturalist who should stick to poetry not politics. These were just some of the labels used to discredit her. Rachel Carson had, in fact, lit a fire on America's chemical landscape.

In speeches before the Garden Club of America and the New England Wildflower Preservation Society, Carson fought back against her detractors and addressed her audiences with great passion. "I recommend you ask yourself—Who speaks?—And Why?" And then again,

Are we being sentimental when we care whether the robin returns to our dooryard and the veery sings in the twilight woods? A world that is no longer fit for wild plants, that is no longer graced by the flight of birds, a world whose streams and forests are empty and lifeless is not likely to be a fit habitat for man himself, for these things are symptoms of an ailing world.

President John F. Kennedy became aware of *Silent Spring* when it was first serialized in the pages of *The New Yorker*. At a press conference on August 29, 1962, a reporter asked Kennedy about the growing concern among scientists regarding dangerous long-term side effects from the use of DDT and other pesticides and whether or not the U.S. Department of Agriculture or the U.S. Public Health Service was planning to launch an investigation into the matter.

"Yes," the President replied. "I think particularly, of course, since Miss Carson's book."

The Life Sciences Panel of the President's Science Advisory Committee was charged with reviewing pesticide use. In 1962, the committee issued a call for legislative measures to safeguard the health of the land and its people against pesticides and industrial toxins. The President's report had vindicated Carson. Her poetics were transformed into public policy.

Rachel Carson testified for over forty minutes during the Hearings before the United States Senate Subcommittee on Reorganization and International Organizations of the Committee on Government Operations, "Interagency Coordination in Environmental Hazards (Pesticides)," on June 4, 1964.

According to Carson's biographer, Linda Lear, "Those who heard Rachel Carson that morning did not see a reserved or reticent woman in the witness chair but an accomplished scientist, an expert on chemical pesticides, a brilliant writer, and a woman of conscience who made the most of an opportunity few citizens of any rank can have to make their opinions known. Her witness had been equal to her vision."

Senator Gruening from Alaska called *Silent Spring* equal to *Uncle Tom's Cabin* in its impact, and predicted it would change the course of history.

In 1967, five years after *Silent Spring* was published, the

Environmental Defense Fund was born, with a mandate, in the words of one its founders, "to build a body of case law to establish a citizen's right to a clean environment." Three years after that, in 1970, the Environmental Protection Agency was established.

And today, we have a new generation of individuals carrying the torch of vigilance forward in the name of ecological integrity: Lois Gibbs, who exposed the Love Canal to the American public as a dark example of industry's arrogance and disregard for the health of communities; Monica Moore and Sarojeni Rengah of Pesticide Action Network who provide scientific data and policy proposals worldwide to citizens fighting to maintain the biological health of their communities.

And women like Mary O'Brien in Eugene, Oregon remind us that the risk assessment question, "How much of this pesticide is 'safe' or 'acceptable'?" is the wrong question to be asking. The better question is, "How little pesticide use is essential?"

These are green patriots who have taken the banner that Rachel Carson raised and have kept it flying high in a world that still refuses to believe in the dangers of biocide.

Tyrone Hayes, the lead researcher on a study concluding that atrazine, the most popular herbicide in the United States, causes a wide range of sexual abnormalities in frogs, was quoted in *The New York Times* on April 17, 2002 as saying, "I'm not saying it's safe for humans. I'm not saying it's unsafe for humans. All I'm saying is that it makes hermaphrodites of frogs."

As Rachel Carson noted,

If...we have concluded that we are being asked to take sense-less and frightening risks, then we should no longer accept the counsel of those who tell us that we must fill our world with poisonous chemicals; we should look about and see what other course is open to us.

Pam Zahoran of Protect Environment and Children Everywhere is showing us an alternative course. She, along with 22,000 other citizens, signed a petition against a major hazardous-waste incinerator to be built by Waste Technologies Industries in East Liverpool, Ohio.

Bill Hedden, former county commissioner in Grand County, Utah, has never given up the hope of seeing 10.5 million tons of radioactive waste removed from the banks of the Colorado River, left from the uranium boom in the 1950's. For almost two decades, he has delivered devastating facts and figures to the United States Congress showing the toxic risks to the entire Colorado River Basin including the Los Angeles water supply.

And Robert Boone, president of the Anacostia Watershed Society, is working with the children of this poverty-stricken community just outside Washington, D.C., to clean up the Anacostia River, one of the most toxic waterways in America. He is restoring hope in this forgotten landscape. So far, they have removed 327 tons of debris, 7,218 tires, and mobilized 25,666 volunteers in their vision of a clean river. They are holding the Environmental Protection Agency accountable to the Clean Water Act.

These are Rachel's sons and daughters who are taking the facts and fueling them with passionate resistance to protect the integrity of their hometowns and communities. This is the bedrock of democracy—"the greatest good for the greatest number for the longest time." By protecting the health of America's open spaces we preserve America's open heart.

Recently, I visited the Rachel Carson National Wildlife Refuge, a rich salt marsh that encompasses approximately 4,500 acres along forty-five miles of coastline in southern Maine. Carson knew this country well and worked toward its protection. It was the place she loved most, the place where she kept summers at her cottage near Boothbay Harbor with her nephew Roger and her dear soulmate, Dorothy Freeman, who lived nearby.

As I walked through the sanctuary and listened to the water songs of red-winged blackbirds and watched the deliberate flight of great blue herons, I wondered, if Carson were alive today, would she find this estuary a bit quieter? Would she find the tidepools less vibrant, vacant of certain creatures? I wondered what accommodations we have made through time without even noticing what we have lost. I would have loved to ask her what price she paid, personally, for her warriorship surrounding *Silent Spring*?

I imagined her looking directly into my eyes, a bit

stunned over such a presumptuous question, shaking her head, and then looking out toward her beloved sea.

Sandra Steingraber, author of *Living Downstream: An Ecologist Looks At Cancer and the Environment*, writes, "Carson laid out five lines of evidence linking cancer to environmental causes.... [She] predicted that the full maturation of whatever seeds of malignancy have been sown by the new lethal agents of the chemical age would occur in the years to come."

The irony is a painful one. Rachel Carson died of breast cancer on April 14, 1964, at the age of fifty-six. Diagnosed in 1960, she wrote *Silent Spring* through her illness and faced her powerful detractors with limited physical strength, often having to be hospitalized after strenuous professional obligations. But the public never knew. She proceeded with great presence and resolve, even completing a rigorous television interview on CBS months before her death, where she was paired with a spokesperson from the chemical industry. Carson's "grace under fire" with compelling facts to back her sentiments finally won public opinion over to her side. Brooks Atkinson in his column in *The New York Times* proclaimed her the winner. He wrote, "Evidence continues to accumulate that she is right and that *Silent Spring* is the 'rights of man' of this generation."

In spite of her cancer, Rachel Carson never lost "the vision splendid" before her eyes. Her love of the natural world, especially all she held dear in the coastal landscape of Maine, sustained and supported her tenacious and elegant spirit.

Before her death, she wrote to her friend, E. B. White, "It is good to know that I shall live on even in the minds of many who do not know me and largely through association with things that are beautiful and lovely."

And she does.

Consider these examples: *Rachel's Daughters*, a film investigating the environmental causes of breast cancer; Rachel's Network, a political organization committed to seeing women in positions of power and leadership within the conservation community; the Rachel Carson Institute at Chatham College dedicated to the awareness and understanding of current environmental issues inspired by their distinguished alumna. And there are thousands of references to Rachel Carson within American culture, including one by a puzzled Richard A. Posner, who wondered in his book, *Public Intellectuals*, why Rachel Carson had more citations in Lexus Nexus than the French Deconstructionist Jacques Derrida. What a perfect metaphor for Rachel Carson's impact. After all, didn't she deconstruct the entire chemical industry until we were able to see, collectively, the essence of what it does—destroy natural systems—the dark toxic roots of pesticides exposed?

Rachel Carson writes, "There is also an ecology of the world in our bodies."

Recently, an open letter was signed and sent to the U.S. Senate to ban reproductive cloning and to place a moratorium on therapeutic cloning by a broad coalition of scientists, environmentalists, feminists, healthcare workers, religious leaders, political leaders, philosophers, and writers. If Rachel Carson were alive, her name would have appeared on that list.

Similar political actions have been taken to elucidate the dangers of genetic engineering, from the possibility of infecting wild salmon populations to the perils of genetically modified foods. Rachel Carson understood that tampering with nature is tampering with health in the broadest, ecological sense.

In 2002, Rachel Carson's spirit is among us. Like her, we can be both fierce and compassionate at once. We can remember that our character has been shaped by the diversity of America's landscape and it is precisely that character that will protect it. We can carry a healthy sense of indignation within us that will shatter the complacency that has seeped into our society in the name of all we have lost, knowing there is still so much to be saved.

Call it sacred rage, a rage grounded in the understanding that all life is intertwined. And we can come to know and continue to learn from the grace of wild things as they hold an organic wisdom that sustains peace.

Do we have the moral courage to step forward and openly question every law, person, and practice that denies justice toward nature?

Do we have the strength and will to continue in this American tradition of bearing witness to beauty and terror which is its own form of advocacy?

And do we have the imagination to rediscover an authentic patriotism that inspires empathy and reflection over pride and nationalism?

Rachel Carson's name is synonymous with courage. She dared to expose the underbelly of the chemical industry and show how it was disrupting the balance of nature. In *Silent Spring* we see her signature strength on the page, and witness how a confluence of poetry and politics with sound science can create an ethical stance toward life.

But perhaps Rachel Carson's true courage lies in her willingness to align science with the sacred, to admit that her bond toward nature is a spiritual one.

I am not afraid of being thought a sentimentalist when I say that I believe natural beauty has a necessary place in the spiritual development of any individual or any society. I believe that whenever we destroy beauty, or whenever we substitute something man-made and artificial for a natural feature of the earth, we have retarded some part of man's spiritual growth.

Rachel Carson has called us to action. *Silent Spring* is a social critique of our modern way of life, as essential to the evolving American ideals of freedom and democracy as anything ever written by our founding fathers.

"If the Bill of Rights contains no guarantee that a citizen shall be secure against lethal poisons distributed either by private individuals or by public officials," Miss Carson wrote, "it is surely only because our forefathers, despite their considerable wisdom and foresight, could conceive of no such problem."

There are many forms of terrorism. Environmental degradation is one of them. We have an opportunity to shift the emphasis on American independence to American interdependence and redefine what acts of responsibility count as heroism. Protecting the lands we love and working on behalf of the safety of our communities from the poisoned residue of corporate and governmental neglect must surely be chief among them. Perhaps this is what the idea of "homeland security" is meant to be in times of terror.

After my father and his friend left, I walked outside and sat on our back porch. The blinking bodies of fireflies were rising and falling above the grasses. They appeared as a company of code-talkers flashing S.O.S. on a very dark night.

References

Brooks, Paul, *House of Life: Rachel Carson At Work*, Houghton Mifflin Co., 1993.

Carson, Rachel
    Silent Spring, Houghton Mifflin Co., 1962 (A special 40th Anniversary Edition of *Silent Spring* will be published in the fall of 2002 by Houghton Mifflin Co.).
    The Edge of the Sea, Houghton Mifflin Co., 1955.
    The Sea Around Us, Oxford University Press, 1951.
    Under the Sea-Wind, Oxford University Press, 1941.

Freeman, Martha (editor), *Always, Rachel: The Letters of Rachel Carson and Dorothy Freeman, 1952 - 1964, The Story of a Remarkable Friendship*, Beacon Press, 1996.

Graham, Frank, *Since Silent Spring*, Houghton Mifflin Co., 1970.

Hynes, Patricia H., *The Recurring Silent Spring*, Elsevier Science Ltd., 1989.

Lear, Linda
    Rachel Carson: Witness For Nature, Henry Holt, 1997.
    Lost Woods: The Discovered Writing of Rachel Carson, Beacon Press, 1999.

Waddell, Craig (editor), *And No Birds Sing: Rhetorical Analyses of Silent Spring*, Southern Illinois University Press, 2000.

Acknowledgements

The Orion Society would like to thank the following individuals and institutions for their generous support of this book:

Brimstone Fund
Jane Lane-Pryor
Hobson Family Foundation
Scott and Ruth Sanders Family Foundation

Terry Tempest Williams would like to acknowledge the influence of Paul Brooks, Roger Cohen, and Deanne Urmy in the essay, "One Patriot." A small portion of this essay originally appeared in "The Spirit of Rachel Carson," published in *Audubon*, July/August, 1992. She would also like to thank Linda Lear, Rachel Carson's biographer, for her meticulous research on the life of Miss Carson.

Barry Lopez's "The Naturalist," originally appeared in

About the Authors

Barry Lopez is the author of fourteen works of fiction and nonfiction, including *Arctic Dreams*, *About This Life*, and *Light Action in the Caribbean*. He is the recipient of the National Book Award, the John Hay Award, Guggenheim and Lannan fellowships, and other honors. He lives and works in Oregon.

Richard Nelson is a nature writer and cultural anthropologist whose work explores the relationships between people and the environment. His books include *Make Prayers to the Raven*, *Shadow of the Hunter*, *Heart and Blood: Living with Deer in America*, and *The Island Within*. He is a recipient of the John Burroughs Medal for nature writing and, in 1999, he was named the Alaska State Writer (Alaska's equivalent to the Poet Laureate). He is also a conservation activist and public wildlands advocate, working for protection of old-growth rainforest in the Tongass National Forest.

Terry Tempest Williams lives in Castle Valley, Utah. Her books include *Refuge: An Unnatural History of Family and Place*; *An Unspoken Hunger*; *Desert Quartet*; *Leap*; and most recently, *Red: Passion and Patience in the Desert*. She is the recepient of a John Simon Guggenheim Fellowship and a Lannan Literary Fellowship in creative nonfiction. Her work has appeared in *The New Yorker*, *The Nation*, *The New York Times*, *Orion*, *Parabola*, and *The Best American Essays*.

The Orion Society

The Orion Society's mission is to inform, inspire, and engage individuals and grassroots organizations across North America in becoming a significant cultural force for healing nature and community. Our programs and publications include:

Orion Magazine: Since 1982, *Orion* has worked to reconnect human culture with the natural world, blending scientific thinking with the arts, engaging the heart and mind, and striving to make clear what we all have in common.

Orion publishes the work of the writers who are shaping a relationship between nature and a new emerging cultural ethic—Barbara Kingsolver, Gary Paul Nabhan,

Sandra Steingraber, David Quammen, Richard Nelson, Terry Tempest Williams, Barry Lopez, Robert Michael Pyle, Thomas Moore, David James Duncan, Wendell Berry, Scott Russell Sanders, Ann Zwinger—as well many new voices.

Orion also includes powerful visual images that blur the boundaries between the human and the natural, and challenge us to see our world from new perspectives. Each issue includes portfolios of paintings and photographs from artists like Frans Lanting, Galen Rowell, Sonya Bullaty, Wolf Kahn, Forrest Moses, and Andy Goldsworthy.

OrionOnline.org: Orion's website features powerful and poignant multimedia content, including web-exclusive articles, videos, and art exhibitions, which are publicized via our popular e-mail updates.

Orion Books: Orion's books range from the popular Nature Literacy Series of educational resources to the New Patriotism Series of essays.

Orion Grassroots Network: The Network encompasses over 500 organizations, diverse in their focus and locale, that are dedicated to healing our fractured relationships with nature and community. To nurture these groups, the Orion Grassroots Network offers a number of strategically created services to ease the isolation of working issue-by-issue by providing a forum where they experience their work as part of the broad movement for cultural change. To learn more: www.oriononline.org/ogn..

The Orion Society is a 501(c)3 nonprofit organization.

Learn more about Orion, or purchase additional copies of *Patriotism and the American Land* or any of our other publications at **www.oriononline.org**

For information on bulk or wholesale orders of *Patriotism and the American Land*, or any of our other publications, please call 888/909-6568.

The Orion Society
187 Main Street, Great Barrington, MA 01230
telephone: 413/528-4422   facsimile: 413/528-0676
email: orion@orionsociety.org   website: www.oriononline.org

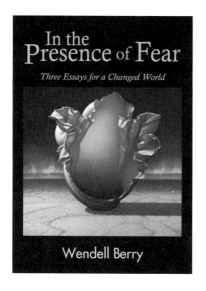